by Iain Gray

Lang**Syne**

PUBLISHING

WRITING *to* REMEMBER

Lang**Syne**

PUBLISHING

WRITING *to* REMEMBER

79 Main Street, Newtongrange,
Midlothian EH22 4NA
Tel: 0131 344 0414   Fax: 0845 075 6085
E-mail: info@lang-syne.co.uk
www.langsyneshop.co.uk

Design by Dorothy Meikle
Printed by Ricoh Print Scotland
© Lang Syne Publishers Ltd 2012

ISBN 978-1-85217-483-5

Booth

MOTTO:
Under this sign thou shalt conquer
(and)
God assists us.

CREST:
A lion holding a laurel
wreath in its right paw.

NAME variations include:
Boothe.

Chapter one:

The origins of popular surnames

by George Forbes and Iain Gray

If you don't know where you came from, you won't know where you're going is a frequently quoted observation and one that has a particular resonance today when there has been a marked upsurge in interest in genealogy, with increasing numbers of people curious to trace their family roots.

Main sources for genealogical research include census returns and official records of births, marriages and deaths – and the key to unlocking the detail they contain is obviously a family surname, one that has been 'inherited' and passed from generation to generation.

No matter our station in life, we all have a surname – but it was not until about the middle of the fourteenth century that the practice of being identified by a particular surname became commonly established throughout the British Isles.

Previous to this, it was normal for a person to be identified through the use of only a forename.

But as population gradually increased and there were many more people with the same forename, surnames were adopted to distinguish one person, or community, from another.

Many common English surnames are patronymic in origin, meaning they stem from the forename of one's father – with 'Johnson,' for example, indicating 'son of John.'

It was the Normans, in the wake of their eleventh century conquest of Anglo-Saxon England, a pivotal moment in the nation's history, who first brought surnames into usage – although it was a gradual process.

For the Normans, these were names initially based on the title of their estates, local villages and chateaux in France to distinguish and identify these landholdings.

Such grand descriptions also helped enhance the prestige of these warlords and generally glorify their lofty positions high above the humble serfs slaving away below in the pecking order who had only single names, often with Biblical connotations as in Pierre and Jacques.

The only descriptive distinctions among the peasantry concerned their occupations, like 'Pierre the swineherd' or 'Jacques the ferryman.'

Roots of surnames that came into usage in England not only included Norman-French, but also Old French, Old Norse, Old English, Middle English, German, Latin, Greek, Hebrew and the Gaelic languages of the Celts.

The Normans themselves were originally Vikings, or 'Northmen', who raided, colonised and eventually settled down around the French coastline.

The had sailed up the Seine in their longboats in 900AD under their ferocious leader Rollo and ruled the roost in north eastern France before sailing over to conquer England in 1066 under Duke William of Normandy – better known to posterity as William the Conqueror, or King William I of England.

Granted lands in the newly-conquered England, some of their descendants later acquired territories in Wales, Scotland and Ireland – taking not only their own surnames, but also the practice of adopting a surname, with them.

But it was in England where Norman rule and custom first impacted, particularly in relation to the adoption of surnames.

This is reflected in the famous *Domesday Book*, a massive survey of much of England and Wales, ordered by William I, to determine who owned what, what it was worth and therefore how much they were liable to pay in taxes to the voracious Royal Exchequer.

Completed in 1086 and now held in the National Archives in Kew, London, 'Domesday' was an Old English word meaning 'Day of Judgement.'

This was because, in the words of one contemporary chronicler, "its decisions, like those of the Last Judgement, are unalterable."

It had been a requirement of all those English landholders – from the richest to the poorest – that they identify themselves for the purposes of the survey and for future reference by means of a surname.

This is why the *Domesday Book*, although written in Latin as was the practice for several centuries with both civic and ecclesiastical records, is an invaluable source for the early appearance of a wide range of English surnames.

Several of these names were coined in connection with occupations.

These include Baker and Smith, while Cooks, Chamberlains, Constables and Porters were to be found carrying out duties in large medieval households.

The church's influence can be found in names such as Bishop, Friar and Monk while the popular name of Bennett derives from the late fifth to mid-sixth century Saint Benedict, founder of the Benedictine order of monks.

The early medical profession is represented by Barber, while businessmen produced names that include Merchant and Sellers.

Down at the village watermill, the names that cropped up included Millar/Miller, Walker and Fuller, while other self-explanatory trades included Cooper, Tailor, Mason and Wright.

Even the scenery was utilised as in Moor, Hill, Wood and Forrest – while the hunt and the chase supplied names that include Hunter, Falconer, Fowler and Fox.

Colours are also a source of popular surnames, as in Black, Brown, Gray/Grey, Green and White, and would have denoted the colour of the clothing the person habitually wore or, apart from the obvious exception of 'Green', one's hair colouring or even complexion.

The surname Red developed into Reid, while

Blue was rare and no-one wanted to be associated with yellow.

Rather self-important individuals took surnames that include Goodman and Wiseman, while physical attributes crept into surnames such as Small and Little.

Many families proudly boast the heraldic device known as a Coat of Arms, as featured on our front cover.

The central motif of the Coat of Arms would originally have been what was borne on the shield of a warrior to distinguish himself from others on the battlefield.

Not featured on the Coat of Arms, but highlighted on page three, is the family motto and related crest – with the latter frequently different from the central motif.

Adding further variety to the rich cultural heritage that is represented by surnames is the appearance in recent times in lists of the 100 most common names found in England of ones that include Khan, Patel and Singh – names that have proud roots in the vast sub-continent of India.

Echoes of a far distant past can still be found in our surnames and they can be borne with pride in commemoration of our forebears.

Chapter two:

High honours

A name of ancient roots, Booth is derived from the Old English 'bothe' and the Scots 'bothie' or 'bothy', indicating someone who lived in a hut or shelter – in particular a herdsman who tended cattle.

Earliest records of the name are found in the northern English region of Yorkshire, in the now redundant form of 'Both' – recorded in Wakefield in 1297.

It is a name that in the British Isles pre-dates by several centuries the Norman Conquest of 1066.

Also of Old Norse roots, its main early presence in England came through the Anglo-Saxons.

Bearers of the Booth name figure prominently in the English historical record.

Born in about 1420, the son of a noted family of Booths that had been settled in Cheshire from earliest times, Lawrence Booth was an important religious and political figure of his day.

Studying civil and canon law at Pembroke Hall, Cambridge, he was later appointed Chancellor of Cambridge University – where he was instrumental in the setting up of its School for the Arts and School of Civil Law.

Appointed Lord Chancellor to Queen Margaret, in 1456 he was also appointed to the powerful post of Keeper of the Privy Seal.

Installed that same year to the influential post of Bishop of Durham, he was later appointed, in 1473, as Lord Keeper of the Privy seal under Edward IV.

He was installed three years later as Archbishop of York, a post he held until his death four years later.

In a later century, Henry Booth, 1st Earl of Warrington, played an important role in what is known as the Glorious Revolution of 1688 that saw the flight into exile of the Catholic James II (James VII of Scotland) and his replacement on the throne by the Protestant William of Orange, as William III, and his wife Mary.

Born in 1652, the politically well connected Booth was a son of George Booth, 1st Baron Delamer, and Lady Elizabeth Grey.

His pedigree also included his maternal grandfather Henry Grey, 1st Earl of Stamford, and his maternal grandmother Anne Cecil, daughter of William Cecil, 2nd Earl of Exeter.

Serving as Member of Parliament (MP) for his native Cheshire between 1678 and 1681, during a period of growing opposition to the rule of the Catholic Stuart dynasty, he became a vociferous advocate of a Protestant monarchy.

Succeeding his father as 2nd Baron Delamer in 1684, his downfall appeared imminent when he was accused of treason for his support of the Monmouth Rebellion in the summer of 1685.

The abortive rebellion took its name from James Scott, 1st Duke of Monmouth, the illegitimate son of Charles II and his mistress Lucy Walter.

Having been forced into exile in Holland, the Protestant Monmouth landed at Lyme Regis, Dorset, in June of 1685 following the accession to the throne of James II.

Issuing a proclamation asserting his right to the throne and with the backing of powerful nobles who included Booth and, in Scotland, Archibald Campbell, 9th Earl of Argyll, Monmouth and a force of up to 4,000 soldiers captured Taunton, in Somerset. But they were defeated on July 5 by the forces loyal to James II at the battle of Sedgemoor.

Monmouth and Argyll, along with other rebel leaders, were captured and executed.

Booth was also tried for treason for his part in the rebellion – but despite the damning evidence against him he managed to secure an acquittal.

With growing opposition to the Catholic rule of James II, William Prince of Orange was invited by a group of powerful figures to invade England from Holland, depose James and secure the throne for himself and his wife Mary – ironically a daughter of the hapless James.

William accordingly landed at Torbay, Devon, in November of 1688 with a force of 20,000 troops.

Simultaneous uprisings took place throughout England, with Henry Booth raising an army on his behalf in Cheshire.

James fled into French exile, while Booth was rewarded by William, following his accession to the throne, with the post of Chancellor of the Exchequer.

Raised to the Peerage as 1st Earl of Warrington, he died in 1694.

Also raised to the Peerage of the United Kingdom, Sir Felix Booth was the immensely wealthy gin distiller born in 1775 in Roydon, Sussex.

The Booth's Gin Company had been founded

in London by his family in 1740, and it was in 1832 that Felix Booth built a distillery in Albany Street, near Regent's Park.

His fortunes further increased when, in 1840, he went into partnership with William Grimble to produce vinegar from the spirit left over from the gin manufacturing process.

Created a Baronet, he died in 1850, while Boothia Peninsula in Canada was named in his honour by the maritime explorer John Ross for having funded his expedition to find the Northwest Passage.

Noted in the Peerage of the United Kingdom in contemporary times is Claire Windsor, Countess of Ulster.

Born Claire Alexandra Booth in 1977 in Sheffield, Yorkshire, and a descendant of the ancient Booth family of Cheshire, she became Countess of Ulster in 2002 through her marriage to Alexander Windsor, Earl of Ulster.

A consultant paediatrician with the General Medical Council, she is also a Fellow of the Royal College of Paediatrics and Child Health.

Chapter three:

Philanthropists and entrepreneurs

One particularly noted English bearer of the Booth name and one whose legacy survives to this day, was the Methodist preacher William Booth – founder and first General of what has become the international humanitarian organisation known as The Salvation Army.

Born in 1829 in Sneinton, Nottingham, he was apprenticed to a pawnbroker at the age of 13 after his father was declared bankrupt.

Converted to the Methodist faith at the age of 15, he began preaching to the poor in his native Nottingham before moving south to London and becoming a full-time preacher for the Methodist Reform Church.

It was in 1865 that he and his wife Catherine, born Catherine Mumford in 1829 in Ashbourne, Derbyshire, founded The Christian Revival Society, later known as The Christian Mission.

Preaching to the poor and dispossessed of

London's East End, The Christian Mission later developed into The Salvation Army, dispensing food to the needy through soup kitchens.

Modelled after the military, The Salvation Army adopted its own quasi-military uniform and, as 'Christian soldiers', its members spread not only the Christian message but also charity to those who were in need of it.

In keeping with its 'army' overtones, William Booth, who died in 1912, became the army's first 'General.'

Despite the charitable ethos of The Salvation Army, its early work was far from easy as it tried to preach the Christian message and warn of the dangers of alcohol.

Catherine Booth later wrote of how her husband would in the early days "stumble home night after night haggard with fatigue, often his clothes were torn and bloody bandages swathed his head where stones had struck."

Known as Mother of the Salvation Army, Catherine Booth died 22 years before her husband, in 1890.

The couple are buried in Abney Park Cemetery, London.

They had eight children, including Bramwell Booth and Ballington Booth, both of whom became prominent in The Salvation Army at an international level.

Catherine Bramwell-Booth, the daughter of Bramwell Booth, who succeeded his father as second general of the organisation, served as one of its commissioners.

Born in 1883, she died at the age of 104 – noted for her organisation of relief work in the aftermaths of both the First and the Second World War, and the recipient of an OBE.

Also noted for his charitable works was the late nineteenth and early twentieth century social reformer and philanthropist Charles Booth.

Born in Liverpool in 1840, his father was a wealthy ship-owner and corn merchant.

Apprenticed to the family business at the age of 16 and inheriting it in 1862 on the death of his father, he expanded it by adding a glove manufacturing enterprise.

Establishing a company with offices not only in his native Liverpool but also in New York, he later set up a steamship company that traded between Liverpool and Brazil.

Despite the vast wealth he accrued, he was also concerned with the plight of the poor and, along with Benjamin Seebohm, was responsible for the compilation of a highly detailed survey documenting working class life in London.

The shocking details of poverty revealed in the survey led to government initiatives to tackle the problem – and to the eventual provision of Old Age Pensions.

Married to Mary Macaulay, a niece of the famous English historian Thomas Macaulay, he died in 1916.

His many works of philanthropy included his gift of the Pre-Raphaelite painter Holman Hunt's famed *The Light of the World to St Paul's Cathedral*, London.

Across the Atlantic from Britain, George Booth was the founder of America's Booth Newspapers chain.

Born in 1864, it was through his marriage to Ellen Scripps, daughter of the newspaper entrepreneur James E. Scripps, that he began a successful career in newspaper publishing.

Through his association with the Scripps organisation, he eventually became owner of the

Evening News Association – now part of the Media News Group, whose many holdings include the *Detroit News*.

In addition to this, along with his two brothers, he founded the independent Booth Newspapers, now part of Advance Publications.

Before his death in 1949, he and his wife founded a number of philanthropic organisations that include Michigan's Cranbrook Educational Community, while they were also benefactors of the Detroit Institute of Arts.

Also in North America, John Booth was the Canadian entrepreneur recognised as a pioneering lumber and railway baron.

Born in 1827 on a farm in Sheffield County, in the Eastern Townships of Quebec, the son of Irish immigrants, his first job was as a carpenter with the Central Vermont Railroad.

Later establishing his own lumber company in Ontario, he won the contract in 1858 to supply the wood for the new Canadian Parliament buildings in Ottawa.

Expanding his lumber business, building Canada's largest sawmill in Ontario, in 1879 he also established the Canada Atlantic Railway from Ottawa to Georgia Bay and, in 1890, completed the Canada Atlantic Railway connecting Ottawa to the United States.

White pine from his lumber yards was also used to build the decks for ocean liners of the Cunard Line; he died in 1925.

One particularly colourful – and ultimately infamous – dynasty of bearers of the Booth name was one founded by the grandly named Junius Brutus Booth.

Born in 1796 in London, and for reasons best known to his parents named after Marcus Junius Brutus, one of the assassins of the Roman Emperor Julius Caesar, it was in 1821 that he abandoned his wife and ran off to the United States with the young flower seller Mary Ann Holmes.

Before deserting his wife in favour of Mary, he had already gained considerable renown in England as an actor, most notably in the title role in an 1817 production of Shakespeare's *Richard III*.

He gained even greater success and adulation reprising the role in his new home of America, along with other roles, but his chaotic behaviour, fuelled by alcohol, took its toll.

Matters became so bad that he would often disappear shortly before sold-out performances and, in the words of one contemporary, would later be found with "ragged, besotted wretches – the greatest actor on the American stage."

He died in 1852 and, in recognition of his great acting skills, was posthumously inducted into the American Theatre Hall of Fame in 1981.

While his erratic nature had ultimately only been of harm to himself, this was not the case with his son John Wilkes Booth, born to Booth and Mary Ann Holmes in Bel Air, Maryland, in 1838.

Named after the eighteenth century English radical politician John Wilkes, he followed in his father's footsteps onto the stage in a production in Baltimore of *Richard III*, playing the role of the Earl of Richmond.

A leading actor by the time of the outbreak of the American Civil War in 1861, Booth became a vehement supporter of the cause of the Confederacy – violently opposed to President Abraham Lincoln's passionate aim of abolishing slavery.

It was over this central issue that the war of 1861 to 1865 was fought, with the Unionist Army of Lincoln ultimately proving victorious.

Booth became increasingly irrational after the fall of the Confederacy.

In what became an extremely complex plot, involving a list of other likeminded characters, it was on April 14th of 1865 that Booth shot Lincoln dead through the back of the head while the unsuspecting President was attending a performance of *Our American Cousin*, in Ford's Theatre, Washington, D.C.

Booth and his co-conspirators fled, but he was tracked down twelve days after the assassination hiding in a barn in Caroline County, Virginia.

It was here that he was shot and killed by a detachment of soldiers from the 16th New York Cavalry Regiment.

His older brother, Edwin Booth, born in 1833, also followed in his father's footsteps by becoming a noted actor.

Appearing beside his father in a production of *Richard III* in the role of Tressel and in other acclaimed productions, his career was blighted for a time following his brother's assassination of Lincoln.

But his fortunes recovered and, before his death in 1893, he managed the Winter Garden Theatre in New York City and had also become the proprietor of the Walnut Street Theatre in Philadelphia.

Chapter four:

On the world stage

The recipient of a star on the Hollywood Walk of Fame, Shirley Booth was the American actress of stage and screen, born Marjory Ford, in Brooklyn, New York, in 1898.

Her Broadway debut came in 1925, while 25 years later she received a Tony Award for her acclaimed role as Lola Delaney in the play *Come Back, Little Sheba*.

Her screen debut came in 1952 with the film adaptation of the play, earning her both an Academy Award and Golden Globe Award for Best Actress.

Emmy Awards came in the early 1960s when she played the title role in the television sitcom *Hazel*; she died in 1992.

Winner of a 2010 Canadian Comedy Award for Film Performance for her role in *Home by Myself*, **Kristin Booth** is the actress born in 1974 in Kitchener, Ontario.

Her other film credits include the 2001 *Jewel* and, from 2006, *Prairie Giant*.

The daughter of a New York Wall Street

broker, **Connie Booth** is the actress, author and psychotherapist born in 1944 in Indianapolis, Indiana.

Married to the English comedian and actor John Cleese from 1968 to 1978, it was with him that she co-wrote the highly popular British television series *Fawlty Towers*, in which they both starred.

Now married to the drama critic John Lahr, she works as a psychotherapist in London.

Born in London in 1992, **Douglas Booth** is the English actor best known for his portrayal of singer Boy George in the 2010 BBC television drama *Worried About the Boy*.

Other television credits include the 2011 *Great Expectations*, while film credits include the 2009 *From Time to Time*.

Best known for his role as Private Henry Hook in the 1964 film *Zulu*, **James Booth** was the stage name of the actor David Greves, born in 1927 in Croydon, Surrey.

Other film credits include *Keeping Mum*, released in the same year as his death in 2005, while television credits include *Coronation Street*, *The Sweeney*, *Auf Wiedersehen Pet* and the American series *Twin Peaks*.

Best known for his role in the BBC television

sitcom *Till Death Us Do Part*, Anthony Booth, better known as **Tony Booth**, is the English actor born in Liverpool in 1931.

Film credits include the 1960 *Suspect* and the 1975 *Brannigan*, which also starred the late John Wayne, while his memoirs include his 2002 *What's Left*.

A staunch supporter of the British Labour Party and former president of the actors' union Equity, he is the father of Cherie Booth, the professional name of the leading lawyer Cherie Blair, who married former British Labour Prime Minister Tony Blair in 1980.

Born in 1954 in Bury, Lancashire, she is patron of the charitable Cherie Blair Foundation and author of the 2008 autobiography *Speaking for Myself*.

Back to the world of entertainment, **George Hoy Booth** was the leading star of British stage and screen of the 1930s and 1940s better known as **George Formby**.

Born in 1904 in Wigan, Lancashire, his father James Booth was also an entertainer.

James Booth used the stage name of 'George Formby', with 'Formby' a town in his native Lancashire – and this was the name his son adopted as a comedy actor, singer and songwriter, accompanying himself on the ukulele banjo.

Born blind, his sight was restored when he was a few months old when a violent coughing fit helped to remove obstructive cauls over his eyes.

Apprenticed as a jockey at the tender age of only seven, it was not until he was aged 17 that he took to the boards of music hall.

Top-selling songs and films followed – including his 1933 songs *With My Little Ukulele in My Hand*, the 1937 *Leaning on a Lamppost* and the 1940 *Count Your Blessings and Smile*.

Awarded an OBE in 1946, he died in 1961, while there is a statue to him in his home town of Wigan.

The writer of a number of classic Hollywood films, **Charles G. Booth** was born in 1896.

Immigrating to America from Britain, he wrote films that include the 1936 *The General Died at Dawn* and the 1941 *Sundown*, while his 1945 *The House on 92nd Street* won him an Academy Award for Best Story.

He died in 1949, while his short story *Caviar for His Excellency* was adapted for the 1988 film *Moon Over Parador*.

Also behind the camera lens, **Margaret Booth** was the acclaimed American film editor born in 1898 in Los Angeles.

Films on which she worked include the 1935 Academy Award-nominated *Mutiny on the Bounty*, the 1973 *The Way We Were* and the 1977 *The Goodbye Girl*.

She died in 2002, the recipient of other awards that include an Academy Honorary Award for her work in film editing and an American Cinema Editors Career Achievement Award.

Bearers of the Booth name have also excelled, and continue to excel, in the highly competitive world of sport.

On the cricket pitch, **Brian Booth** is the former middle-order Australian batsman, born in 1933 in Bathurst, New South Wales, who played 29 Tests for Australia between 1961 and 1966, captaining the team from 1965 to 1966.

On the fields of European football, **Tommy Booth** is the English former footballer who was capped four times for England at Under-23 level. Born in 1949 in Middleton, Lancashire, he played for teams that include Manchester City and Preston North End – managing the latter from 1985 to 1986.

The holder of 22 caps for playing with the Scotland national team, **Scott Booth** is the former striker who now works as a pundit for BBC Sport.

Born in Aberdeen in 1971, teams he played for include Aberdeen and German team Borussia Dortmund.

In the sport of ice hockey, **David Booth** is the American professional player who has played for teams that include the Vancouver Canucks and Florida Panthers in the National Hockey League (NHL).

Born in 1984, he has also represented his nation at Under-18 and Under-20 championship level.

In basketball, **Calvin Booth** is the American former player who was a member of the U.S. team that won the gold medal at the 1998 Goodwill Games in New York and the 2001 games in Brisbane.

Born in 1976 in Reynoldsburg, Ohio, he played from 1999 to 2009 for teams that include the Dallas Mavericks, Minnesota Timberwolves and Sacramento Kings.

From sport to the written word, **Stephen Booth** is the English crime novelist whose 2000 *Black Dog* won a Barry Award for Best British Crime Novel.

Born in 1952 in Burnley, Lancashire, his series of crime novels feature the Derbyshire detectives Cooper and Fry.

The founder of the Sceptre Press, **Martin Booth** was the novelist and poet born in 1944 in Lancashire.

His 1944 novel *A Very Private Gentleman* was adapted for film six years after his death in 2004 as *The American*, starring George Clooney.

A noted English travel writer, **Alan Booth** was born in 1946 in London.

Best known for travel books on Japan that include his 1985 *The Roads to Sata*, he died in 1993.

In the world of publishing, **Mary Louise Booth** was the distinguished editor, writer and translator born in 1831 in what is now Yaphank, New York.

A translator into English of the works of French language authors and the editor of *Harper's Bazaar* magazine since its launch in 1867, she died in 1889.

In the equally creative world of art, **Franklin Booth** was the American artist and illustrator whose work appeared in magazines ranging from *Harper's Bazaar* and *Good Housekeeping* to *Cosmopolitan*.

Born in 1874 in Carmel, Indiana, he became

noted for his highly detailed pen and ink illustrations which also featured on iconic advertisements for Rolls-Royce, Bulova Watches and Paramount Pictures.

His artistic talents were put to use during the First World War through his illustration of recruitment posters and, rather macabrely – death certificates for American soldiers killed on the Western Front; he died in 1948.

Bearers of the Booth name have also been noted for inventive talent.

Born in 1918 in Weybridge, Surrey, **Andrew Booth** was the British electrical engineer, physicist and scientist who pioneered the technique of 'magnetic drum memory' for early computers.

He also gave his name to Booth's Multiplication Algorithm for use in complex mathematical physics, while he also carried out work in the field of crystallography which laid the basis for the first electronic computers in the United Kingdom.

Working latterly at Birbeck College, University of London, he died in 2009.

Not only the designer of Royal Navy battleships, suspension bridges and Ferris wheels for amusement parks in London, Vienna and Paris,

Hubert Booth was the British engineer, born in Gloucester in 1871 and who died in 1955, who invented the first powered vacuum cleaner.

It was after seeing a demonstration of a compressed air cleaning system in London's St Pancras station for use in railway carriages that he hit upon the idea of a device to suck air through a filter.

The invention was duly patented in 1910, with the vacuum cleaners produced by Fielding and Platt of Gloucester.

But with Booth's design more suited for industrial rather than commercial use, it was soon overtaken by the Hoover Company of America.

All modern vacuum cleaners are nevertheless based on Booth's original concept.